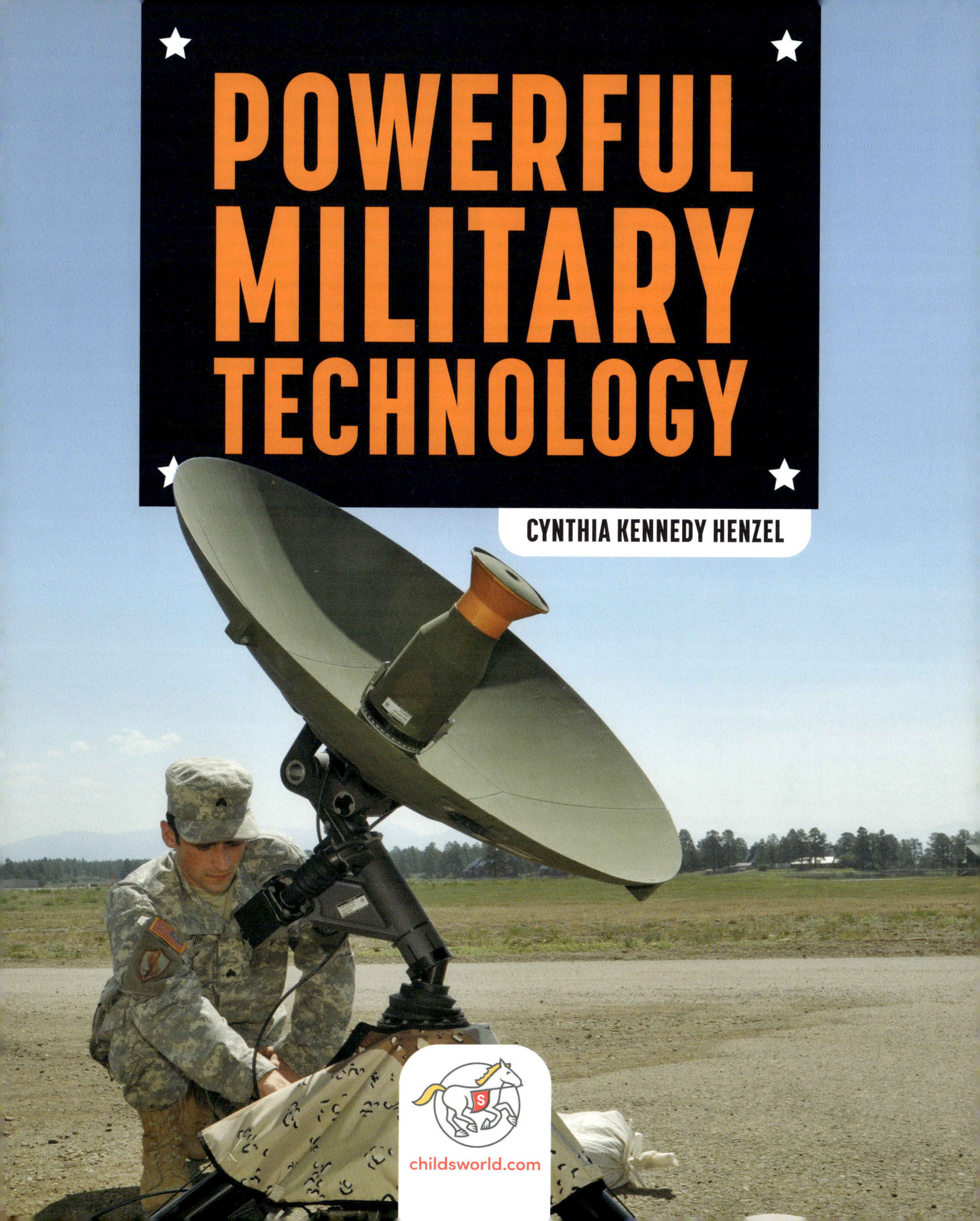
POWERFUL MILITARY TECHNOLOGY
CYNTHIA KENNEDY HENZEL
childsworld.com

Published by The Child's World®
800-599-READ • www.childsworld.com

Photography Credits
Photographs ©: Tech. Sgt. Wolfram Stumpf/Colorado National Guard/US Air National Guard/DVIDS, cover, 1; 94th Airlift Wing/Secretary of the Air Force Public Affairs/US Air Force/DVIDS, 3, 5; Northrop Grumman/US Air Force, 6; Petty Officer 1st Class Bryan Niegel/US Navy/DVIDS, 7; Cpl. Danielle Rodrigues/49th Wing Public Affairs/US Air Force/DVIDS, 9 (top); Master Sgt. Eric Harris/US Air Force, 9 (top middle); Tech. Sgt. Emerson Nuñez/100th Air Refueling Wing Public Affairs/US Air Force/DVIDS, 9 (bottom middle); Master Sgt. Jeremy Lock/Defense Imagery Management Operations Center/DVIDS, 9 (bottom); Airman 1st Class Jared Lovett/86th Airlift Wing/Public Affairs/US Air Force/DVIDS, 11; STR/Presidency/AP Images, 12; Amy Smith/US Navy/DVIDS, 15; Lance Cpl. Alejandro Bedoya/Marine Corps Air Ground Combat Center, Twentynine Palms/DVIDS, 16; R.J. Oriez/90th Missile Wing Public Affairs/US Air Force/DVIDS, 19; US Navy/DVIDS, 20

ISBN Information
9781503816701 (Reinforced Library Binding)
9781503881402 (Portable Document Format)
9781503882713 (Online Multi-user eBook)
9781503884021 (Electronic Publication)

LCCN 2022951204

Printed in the United States of America

ABOUT THE AUTHOR

Cynthia Kennedy Henzel has a BS in social studies education and an MS in geography. She has worked as a teacher-educator in many countries. Currently, she writes fiction and nonfiction books and develops education materials for social studies, history, science, and ELL students. She has written more than 90 books and 150 stories for young people.

CONTENTS

CHAPTER ONE

INVISIBLE AIRCRAFT

People gather outside an aircraft **hangar** in California. In front of the crowd, a huge aircraft is covered by a white sheet. It is dark outside. Blue lights shine behind the aircraft. It is December 2, 2022. The US military is about to introduce its newest bomber.

The lights get brighter. Slowly, the sheet is pulled back. The crowd begins to cheer. "Ladies and gentlemen," a voice announces, "our nation's B-21 Raider."

The B-21 is a sleek aircraft. It has long wings. The **cockpit** does not rise far above the aircraft. Much of the B-21's design was still secret when it was unveiled. But drawings of the aircraft showed that it has a batwing shape. The front of the aircraft is shaped like a large V. The back is shaped like a W.

When the B-21 Raider was announced, the US Air Force said it planned to buy at least 100 of them. Each aircraft costs more than $600 million.

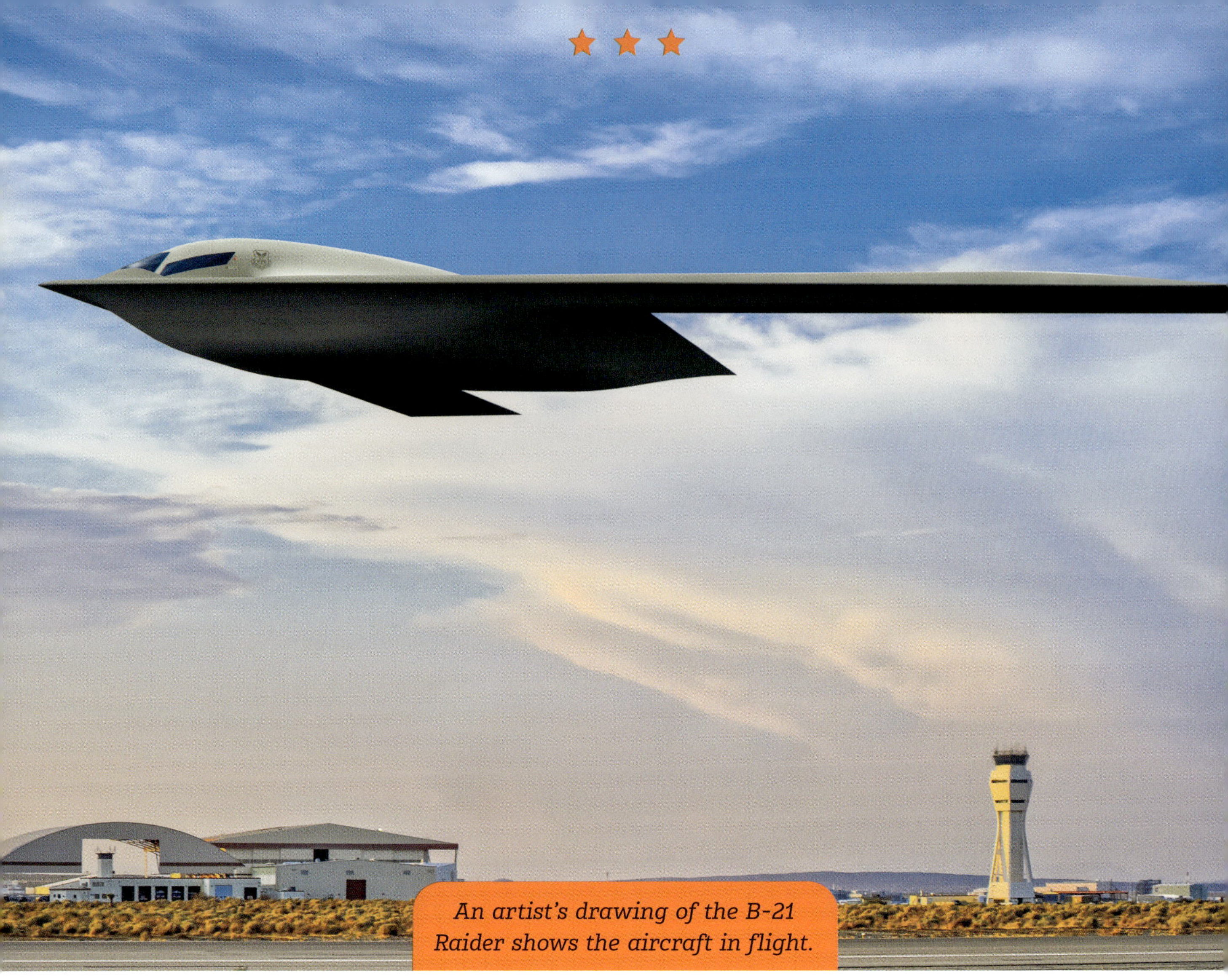

An artist's drawing of the B-21 Raider shows the aircraft in flight.

US military personnel announce that the B-21 Raider is the country's newest stealth bomber. Stealth technology helps aircraft stay hidden from enemies. Until 2022, the B-2 Spirit was the most advanced stealth bomber in the US military. The B-21 is similar in design. But new developments make the B-21 even more stealthy.

Radar is a system of equipment that shows the location of nearby objects. It sends out signals. It then detects the reflection of those signals after they bounce off objects. The B-21 is nearly invisible to enemy radar. Its front edge and cockpit are curved. The wings are flat and angled. This shape reflects signals away from the radar's sensors.

Aircraft that don't use stealth technology are more easily detected by radar.

The material of stealth bombers also absorbs radar signals. Parts of the B-2 Sprit are covered in special paint that helps with stealth. After each flight, someone checks the B-2's wings. Small cracks can ruin the aircraft's stealth. The B-21 Raider's material is still top secret. But officials say its coating is even more high-tech. This coating will also be easier to maintain.

Stealth technology also helps aircraft stay cool. Aircraft engines get very hot. Enemies may be able to detect planes using heat sensors. Heat-seeking missiles can also aim themselves toward hot engines. But stealth bombers cool the hot air from their engines before it leaves the plane. This makes the aircraft harder to detect.

The dramatic reveal of the B-21 Raider was a big step forward for the US military. But the stealth technology of the B-21 is only one kind of powerful military technology. Many new defense and weapons systems are being developed, too.

Stealth aircraft use special technology to avoid enemy detection. The shape and material of these aircraft are especially important.

STEALTH AIRCRAFT FEATURES

The F-117 Nighthawk, a retired stealth aircraft, used a material called iron ball paint to absorb radar signals.

Every surface on the B-2 Spirit is curved to send radar signals away from sensors.

Vents on top of the B-2 direct air from the engine away from heat sensors below.

Radar waves could detect the pilot through the windshield of the F-22 Raptor. So the cockpit is covered in a reflective coating to deflect radar waves.

CHAPTER TWO

CYBER WARFARE

Cyber security and cyber warfare are important to the US military. Cyber warfare means using technology to attack a country's computer systems. Cyber attacks can be just as dangerous as missiles or bombs. Cyber security protects against these attacks.

Militaries and governments store important information on computers. **Hackers** are people who try to steal that information. Enemies could learn about secret technology, plans of attack, or security weaknesses. Aircraft, ships, and missiles also use computers to navigate and communicate. Cyber warfare can **disrupt** these systems. It can make radar and missile defense systems stop working, too. Such attacks would leave a country without military weapons or defenses.

Troops learn about cyber security. They are trained to detect and prevent cyber threats.

The Stuxnet worm attacked computers at the Natanz nuclear facility in Iran.

One of the first major cyber attacks was the Stuxnet worm. It was discovered in 2010. Many people believe it was created by the US government. Stuxnet disrupted Iran's nuclear weapons program. Nuclear weapons are the most dangerous weapons on Earth. The US government has tried to prevent Iran from developing them.

Stuxnet was a harmful kind of software. Software controls how computers work. The Stuxnet software found out which computers ran the nuclear weapons equipment. It then sent instructions for the equipment to damage itself. This cyber attack wasn't detected until it had damaged hundreds of machines. Experts say this attack set Iran's nuclear program back by about two years.

The US takes cyber security very seriously. The US Cyber Command is part of the Department of Defense. Its job is to protect the United States from cyber attacks. This team makes US military systems more secure. These systems are almost impossible to hack. The team also searches for cyber threats.

Cyber warfare takes months or years of planning. Hackers must get into computer systems without being noticed. Then they must wait until the right time to launch the attack. Cyber threat hunters look for any signs of cyber weapons in US systems. Then the US Cyber Command can get rid of the threats before they attack.

New types of cyber warfare can attack advanced computer systems. But cyber security has become more advanced, too. New technology will continue to protect the US military from cyber threats.

CHAPTER THREE

NEW WEAPONS

The US military develops many kinds of weapons. These advanced weapons are very powerful. It is hard for enemies to defend against them. Some weapons are deadly. Others protect troops without being deadly.

Hypersonic missiles are a new kind of cruise missile. Cruise missiles fly at a low **altitude**. They can steer themselves toward a target. But hypersonic missiles are much faster. They can move at more than five times the speed of sound. That's more than 3,800 miles per hour (6,120 kmh). The speed of these missiles makes them very hard to track or destroy. This ability would make it difficult for enemies to defend against US attacks.

THE KINZHAL MISSILE

The first use of hypersonic missiles on a battlefield was in Ukraine. Russia invaded Ukraine in February 2022. In March, Russia fired a number of its Kinzhal hypersonic missiles into Ukrainian territory. The Kinzhal missile has a range of 1,243 miles (2,000 km). It flies at ten times the speed of sound.

The US military tests new hypersonic missiles during the development of these high-tech weapons.

Missiles use explosives to destroy targets. But directed energy weapons, such as lasers, use a powerful beam of energy instead. High-power lasers are extremely dangerous. They are silent and travel at the speed of light. Lasers don't need to be reloaded. They don't run out of **ammunition** as long as they have power. These features allow lasers to quickly destroy targets without detection.

The Active Denial System has a large plate. Energy reflects off this plate and is shot out as a beam.

The US Navy started using one of the first high-power laser systems in August 2022. Several US battleships received the HELIOS system. HELIOS has a powerful laser that can destroy targets. These lasers can shoot down drones or anti-ship missiles. Drones are aircraft that are controlled with a remote and have no people on board. HELIOS can also dazzle enemy radar by using a laser to blind their sensors. Dazzling makes it hard for enemies to track the ship.

The military has also developed lasers that are not **lethal**. The Active Denial System is used to protect areas or disrupt enemy activities. It shoots a beam of energy that can hit targets up to 3,280 feet (1,000 m) away. The system uses a specific kind of energy. When the beam hits a person, it causes the person's skin to feel as if it is burning. But the laser causes no permanent harm. It does not harm other things in the area, either. This technology is not deadly, but it helps protect US troops and push away enemies.

CHAPTER FOUR

PROTECTING THE COUNTRY

The United States is not the only country developing advanced weapons. These new tools can also be used against the United States. The US military must develop systems to defend against attacks.

Intercontinental ballistic missiles (ICBMs) are made to hit targets that are far away. The United States could hit a target anywhere on Earth with an ICBM. Today, countries such as North Korea are developing ballistic missiles. This development puts the United States in danger. New technology helps protect the United States from ballistic missiles.

An Air Force Base in Wyoming displays three ICBMs: a Peacekeeper (left), Minuteman III (middle), and Minuteman I (right).

US AIR FORCE
US AIR FORCE
US AIR FORCE

The Aegis Ballistic Missile Defense system launches missiles from ships.

The Missile Defense Agency created the Aegis Ballistic Missile Defense system for Navy ships. This system defends against short- to mid-range missiles. Aegis uses radar to detect and track an incoming missile. It has **interceptors** to destroy the missile in the air. If Aegis detects a missile, it tells other Navy ships through the command and control system. Dozens of US ships are armed with Aegis systems. These systems protect US coasts. They help protect US **allies**, too.

On land, the Ground-based Midcourse Defense (GMD) system defends the entire United States. It can protect against mid- to long-range missiles. Like Aegis, GMD tracks ballistic missiles and intercepts them. There is one GMD base in California and another in Alaska. The systems fire interceptors at incoming missiles. In the air, the interceptor communicates with the command and control systems to find and destroy ballistic missiles. Together, the GMD and Aegis systems protect the United States.

The US military is constantly developing new technology. Stealth aircraft like the B-21 allow the US Air Force to fly nearly undetected. Cyber warfare can be used to harm enemies through their computer systems. New weapons provide US troops with powerful tools, both lethal and nonlethal. Defense systems protect against long-range missiles. All these technologies help keep the United States safe.

DRONE DEFENSE

Military drones carry weapons such as bombs. They can also be used to gather information. Drone defense systems use radar, cameras, and microphones to detect enemy drones. They can shoot down enemy drones with missiles. Technology can also interrupt the connection between drones and their pilots. Some systems even let US pilots take control of enemy drones.

GLOSSARY

allies (AL-lyze) Allies are countries whose militaries are on the same side. The US military shares technology with its allies.

altitude (AL-tih-tood) Altitude measures how high up in the air something is. The cruise missile flew at an altitude of 100 to 300 feet (30–90 m).

ammunition (am-yoo-NIH-shun) Ammunition is a supply of bullets. Lasers need only energy, not regular ammunition.

cockpit (KOK-pit) The cockpit is the part of an aircraft where the pilot sits. The B-21 Raider's cockpit does not rise far above the aircraft.

cyber (SY-bur) Cyber means that something is related to computers. Cyber weapons attack computer systems.

disrupt (dis-RUPT) Disrupt means to interrupt an event or action. Cyber warfare can disrupt how a computer functions.

hackers (HAK-urz) Hackers are people who gain access to computer systems and information that they shouldn't be able to access. Hackers found secret attack plans on the enemy's computer.

hangar (HANG-uhr) A hangar is a large building where aircraft are stored. The B-21 Raider was kept in a hangar.

interceptors (in-tur-SEHP-turs) Interceptors are fast missiles that defend against enemy attacks. Crews fired the interceptors in time to destroy the enemy missile.

lethal (LEE-thul) Lethal means that something uses enough force to cause death. Many missiles are lethal weapons.

FAST FACTS

- Stealth technology helps aircraft stay hidden from enemies. The B-21 Raider is a stealth bomber in the US military.
- Cyber warfare attacks enemies through their computer systems. The Stuxnet worm was a powerful cyber weapon that hurt Iran's nuclear weapons program.
- Hypersonic missiles are incredibly powerful weapons. They can fly at more than five times the speed of sound.
- Lasers are quiet, fast, and powerful weapons. They are hard for enemies to detect. The Active Denial System is a nonlethal laser.
- The Aegis Ballistic Missile Defense system and the Ground-based Midcourse Defense system protect the United States and its allies from incoming ballistic missiles.

ONE STRIDE FURTHER

- New technology allows aircraft to be stealthier. What kinds of missions do you think need stealth aircraft the most? Why?
- Cyber security is more important now than ever. What kind of information do you think enemies are looking for on US computer systems? How can the US military keep that information safe?
- The military is always developing new weapons. What kind of weapons do you think it should invent next? How would these weapons be useful?

FIND OUT MORE

IN THE LIBRARY

Hamen, Susan E. *Military Technology.* Parker, CO: The Child's World, 2024.

Mapua, Jeff. *Working with Tech in the Military.* New York, NY: Rosen, 2020.

Noll, Elizabeth. *Stealth Technology.* Minneapolis, MN: Bellwether Media, 2022.

ON THE WEB

Visit our website for links about military technology:
childsworld.com/links

Note to Parents, Caregivers, Teachers, and Librarians: We routinely verify our Web links to make sure they are safe and active sites. So encourage your readers to check them out!

INDEX